Experience Job Satisfaction
Your Roadmap to Professional Fulfillment

By Teri Aulph

© Copyright 2010, Teri Aulph

All rights reserved.

No part of this book may be reproduced, stored in a retrieval system, or transmitted by any means, electronic, mechanical, photocopying, recording, or otherwise, without written permission from the author.

ISBN: 978-0-88144-023-2

What People Are Saying

"Teri provides practical guidance and insights in navigating the workplace relationship minefield. Her insights are both credible and on-target from true-life experiences in the corporate world. She brings a fresh approach to career coaching that bridges the often conflicting needs of career and personal fulfillment."

Patrick Gallagher
Former Vice President, Engineering
BorgWarner, Inc.

"A compilation of articles like this is an incredible resource for anyone in the middle of a job search, exploring next career opportunities, leveraging strengths or simply looking for advice on how to navigate a work-related issue or problem. Teri's background and expertise makes this the perfect quick-reference guide for anyone."

Denise Reid
Director Talent Strategies & Recruitment
Tulsa Metro Chamber

"Teri Aulph's leadership journey and business experience uniquely positions her to speak into today's environment. You will see it in her writing; she knows people are the true key to any company or organization's success. Teri will make a difference in your thinking. As you read *Experience Job Satisfaction* you will want more of her influence on your company."

Steve Laswell, CSC
The People Developer
Next Level Executive Coaching, LLC

"Teri is a true professional and leader who instills a sense of competence and confidence with each contact. Teri has a rich background and brings outstanding direction, extensive experience, and business intelligence to any given assignment. But of equal importance are her incredible soft skills. Teri conveys empathy, integrity, humor, and a sense of team to her projects and her clients are enriched and enlightened by the experience."

Gail Hay, PHR
Sr. Vice President and COO
Market Planning Solutions, Inc.

"Our organization utilizes Teri Aulph Consulting LLC for a wide range of Human Resources services. Teri goes beyond the traditional role of an HR consultant. She has the unique ability to integrate herself into the organization and serve as your strategic HR business partner. Teri thoroughly assesses and understands the needs of her clients and tailors custom solutions to effectively meet their specific needs. Her knowledge and experience are unsurpassed and she exemplifies professionalism, integrity and superior customer service. *Experience Job Satisfaction* is a reflection of her expertise."

Jennifer Fennema
HR Business Partner – Department of Utility Services
City of Henderson, Nevada
Formerly Director, HR, Atlas Pipeline

"Competition for the best jobs is fierce, but Teri's global experience in Talent Management will put you a step ahead in the talent race! She has taken her experience in coaching executives at the Fortune 500 level and turned it into a book you can use to take your career to the next level! Use her wealth of knowledge to land a better job, a bigger raise, and a better understanding of what it takes to play in the corporate big leagues!"

Kelly Riggs, Author
1-on-1 Management™: What Every Great Manager Knows That You Don't
Vmax Performance Group

"What sets Teri apart from other HR Coaches is her passion to keep abreast of the latest trends in the industry and leverage her knowledge to serve those who she coaches. In today's world of high unemployment, it takes a great career coach who can both teach and motivate a jobseeker in bringing out their ability to showcase their best attributes to employers- not always an easy task."

Jeffrey Garber
Founder & CEO, 360JobInterview

"Teri Aulph is so accomplished in so many areas that we really need to use her as a "role model" for many roles that are important in our community today. An excellent "change agent.""

Mel Bost
PMO Expert

"Teri brings energy, creativity and a rich depth of experience to any project. She has experience with very large companies in organizational development, leadership development and talent management but she can make that experience practical and applicable down to the smallest of companies. I respect Teri and her experience and take her advice and consultation whenever I can get it."

Mike Henry, Sr.
Leadership Development Coach
President, Lead Change Group

"Where others see "resources" – indistinct and interchangeable – Teri sees unique personalities, distinct talents, unrealized potential. Teri puts relationships first. She has an ability to "connect" with people unlike any I've ever seen, to find in others talent and skills they may never have seen in themselves, and then to connect them with the opportunities that reveal and maximize that potential. Teri will be an invaluable asset – and a transformative one — to any organization that is fortunate enough to attract her attention. I can think of few people from whom I've learned more."

T.J. Sexton
Client Systems Specialist
Contributor, Innovation Lab
Community Action Project

"As is evident in the Leadership section of *Experience Job Satisfaction*, Leadership begins as a way of being, not a way of commanding."

S. Max Brown, CRP
Vice President of Organizational Learning
Rideau Recognition Management Institute

More than ever business leaders are finding that this is an 80/20 world: 20% of your employees do 80% of the work, 20% of the managers are responsible for 80% of the firm's profits and future managers, 20% of an employee's time leads to 80% of their productivity and so on goes Pareto Rule in business. Teri understands these principals and applies fundamental concepts to provide leaders and employees with powerful, easy to use ideas and concepts to break apart traditional business constraints and increase productivity in the workplace.

Robert H Bond
The StrenghtsCoach.org
Changing Children's Lives for a more Positive Future

Dedication

This book is dedicated to the men and women seeking jobs, may you find a place to contribute and continue your journey as a satisfied and fulfilled employee. This book is also dedicated to employees everywhere who make efforts every day to raise the bar on performance.

"Our chief want is someone who will inspire us to be what we know we could be."

Ralph Waldo Emerson

Table of Contents

Table of Contents ix

Why Read This Book? xiii

Acknowledgements xv

Forward xvii

Introduction xix

You Want This Book If… xix

How This Book Is Organized xxi

Section 1   Step Up And Take Ownership Of Your Career 1

    Chapter 1   Create Your Own Rearview Mirror 3

    Chapter 2   Set Yourself Apart 5

    Chapter 3   Networking Advice from Networking Guru, Peter Biadasz 7

    Chapter 4   11 Ways To Lose Your Job 10

    Chapter 5   Are You Management Material? 12

    Chapter 6   5 Reasons To Quit Your Job 14

Chapter 7	Take Care Of You	16
Section 2	Are You Where You're Supposed To Be?	19
Chapter 8	Culture Assimilation	21
Chapter 9	Tweets, Twibes And Tweeples	23
Chapter 10	You're Fired!	25
Chapter 11	Brick & Mortar vs. No Boundaries, Part 1	28
Chapter 12	Brick & Mortar vs. No Boundaries, Part 2	33
Section 3	Be Fierce About Your Job Search	39
Chapter 13	10 Updates To Improve Your Resume	41
Chapter 14	Before You Enter An Interview, Arm Yourself With A Compelling Story	45
Chapter 15	Are The Unemployed Being Snubbed?	47
Chapter 16	Strong Fit Or Misfit?	49
Chapter 17	15 Topics Smart Job Seekers Never Discuss	51
Section 4	Define Yourself As A Leader	53
Chapter 18	Leaders Who Coach	55
Chapter 19	Leadership For Growth	58
Chapter 20	The Framework Of Effective Leadership	61
Section 5	Risks & Rewards Of Workplace Relationships	63
Chapter 21	You Landed The Job! Now What?	65

Chapter 22	Dear Boss, ... 68
Chapter 23	Dear Bob, ... 70
Chapter 24	Generational Differences, Do They Matter? 72
Chapter 25	To: Employees 74
Chapter 26	Dysfunctional Boss, Part 1 76
Chapter 27	Dysfunctional Boss/Employee Relationships, Part 2 79
Chapter 28	The Implications Of A Work Spouse, Part 1 81
Chapter 29	The Implications Of A Work Spouse, Part 2 83

About The Author 85

Why Read This Book?

Rarely does a day go by that I do not receive a call from someone who either needs assistance with a work-related issue or is requesting help managing a job search. It is not uncommon to be pulled aside in a meeting to be asked how to position for a promotional opportunity or how to prepare for a performance evaluation. It became clear to me that there are people everywhere who desire guidance on job related issues.

Over a year ago I began writing for a couple of organizations. I write a career article for an online publication and use the venue as a way to provide suggestions and guidance to people everywhere. I often use my real-life experiences to determine the topics and I have found that people all over the world share very similar experiences.

My readership has grown into the thousands and I found myself participating in a virtual community of people interested in enhancing their careers. Essentially, everyone wants to find satisfaction and fulfillment in the work they choose to do.

This book is a compilation of the articles that received the most comments or were re-published most frequently. There are plenty of career books from which to choose. It is my intent to provide readers with information that is based on real experiences presented with authenticity.

I have written this book keeping in mind the many extraordinary people of who have crossed through my life. My desire is to provide real solutions in an applicable context to assist anyone who is experiencing a difficult struggle in the workplace.

More times than not, people feel they cannot share work-related issues with their peers at work. They don't want to compromise their employment and fear their issue will be misunderstood. I have taken this opportunity to leverage my 15+ years of Human Resources experience in large companies by sharing strategies and practical advice.

If you are interested in improving, changing or assessing your career, you should read this book.

Acknowledgements

To Josh and Brady, I am forever grateful for your ongoing love, compassionate understanding and unwavering support in every endeavor I embark upon. I value our mutual respect for one another and genuine care and concern. The gift of being your mother is and will always be my favorite role. Much appreciation goes to Ashley for taking time out of your very busy schedule to assist with my book. You are an inspiration.

Thank you, Peter, for making my wishful thinking a reality. I appreciate your patience with my timeline and your guidance along the journey.

To my clients, colleagues, family, friends and Zumba buddies, please know your support means everything.

Forward

In the world economic situation of today, everything is changing. Jobs and industries as a whole are dying, being replaced by new jobs and new industries. The constant advancement in technologies has changed the landscape of not only the job market available, but how one goes about seeking new opportunities.

Long gone are the days of sending a resume to a company and waiting for a call for an interview and we're not talking about sending a resume via fax or snail mail. We're talking about sending a resume by email. Sending a resume to a position posted on a job board will often end up in a black hole, where you never receive a response.

With unemployment at record levels, one needs to distinguish themselves from the competition. The advancements in technology networking sites, such as LinkedIN, has given employment seekers a lot more tools at their disposal.

Teri Aulph is an industry expert, providing advice on talent management and the link between people and a successful company. Teri has extensive experience working for Fortune 500 companies, as an HR leader. Make no mistake; people are the most important factor in a company's success.

In today's market, people need to look at a job search as a job itself. You must utilize all of your resources and advice from career coaches. Networking, working with recruiters and industry experts are vital parts of landing your dream job. Everything from asking the right questions to how to improve your resume are necessary steps for any individual looking for a new opportunity. However, your "job" does not end once you land a new opportunity; there are nuances to creating a better work environment for yourself.

Teri and her years of industry experience give you an extensive breakdown of how to create your career plan.

Kevin Raxter
Vice-President
The Centrics Group
www.thecentricsgroup.com

Author of:
Staffing: Recruiting with New Tricks and Old Techniques
http://kevinraxterbook.com/

Introduction

You Want This Book If...

You feel stuck in your current job and want to proactively make a change.

You want to stop being a victim to your boss.

You are a job seeker and can't seem to step across the interview threshold.

You are considering a job change to a virtual company and want to better understand how it works.

You seem to always be behind and often feel overwhelmed.

You feel you have lost control of your career and want to feel that 'excited' feeling again.

You have found yourself back in the market for the first time in over 10 years and have no idea what to do first.

You want to remain current regarding career issues.

You are a leader in your organization and recently looked behind you to find nobody is following.

You are a leader and have compromised your basic principals due to pressure.

You think you may have a Work Spouse and have no idea how to get out of it.

You work with someone who has a Work Spouse and it is driving you crazy.

How This Book Is Organized

Section 1 provides information and tools in a step-by-step process you can use to stay at the top of your game, as well as strategies to position your career for success.

Section 2 guides you through various company structures focused on how the culture of an organization impacts the way it does business and the people involved. This information will guide you in assessing the type of culture in which you will be the most fulfilled.

Section 3 is grounded in practical advise on how to stand out in a sea of job candidates by writing a 'best practice' resume and equipping yourself to ace the job interview.

Section 4 focuses on leadership describing different models that have proven to be most effective and describes how to measure your leadership effectiveness.

Section 5 reveals the risks and rewards of various workplace relationships and the results of mismanaging them.

Step Up And Take Ownership Of Your Career

"I'm not afraid of storms, for I'm learning to sail my ship."

Louisa May Alcott

Create Your Own Rearview Mirror

If an opportunity arose tomorrow that meant upward mobility for you and you were requested to compile a list of your measureable accomplishments for the past 12 months – would you be able to put this together easily?

Most people would have to access the calendars on their computers, Blackberries, iphones, dig in their desk drawer for old post-its, check their LinkedIn profiles, ask colleagues, etc. In the end, they would be able to put something together that would most likely be incomplete, thus, selling themselves short.

In the fast-paced work environments we are living in, we move from one deadline to the other always looking ahead. We spend little time documenting our day-to-day activities, successes and less than ideal results. As a result, we are depriving ourselves of the value of learning from results that miss the mark, as well as successes.

I was fortunate early in my career to have a mentor that required me to carry a journal at all times. The intent was to date the top of each page and document phone calls, meeting notes, and general events throughout the day. This was very useful as I was learning the position, the company, and how people fit into the organization. After a few months, I found myself referring back to my notes on a regular basis, which certainly gave me an advantage.

A few years later, I discovered I had created a rearview mirror of my career – good, bad and indifferent. It chronicled my work-life events, along with all the relationships. I began taking a few minutes at the end of each day to scribe what went well, what didn't go well and what I learned from each. In review, it showed trends in my work behavior and highlighted events that may have seemed benign at the time, but ultimately had high impact. It also reminded me of those who went before me, who led me, who pushed me and who got in my way...all important as we define who we are and who we want to be.

Documenting mileposts as you journey through your career path will provide you historical data, as well as invaluable lessons unique to your career. A work journal is a small monetary investment that can result in a substantial investment in you. It is never too late to start writing your story.

Set Yourself Apart

Are you a new college grad, new to a company or in a new position or industry? All these scenarios require you to understand clearly what you want, hone your peripheral vision, and become fearless regarding what you are willing to take on.

Gone are the days of the traditional 8 to 5 workday. If you want to set yourself apart and be poised for the next level up, you have to leverage your strengths. Recognizing and seizing opportunities others may not will communicate you are focused on succeeding. Going with the flow, however, will not differentiate you from the masses.

At the beginning of a new experience, it is important to get up to speed as quickly as possible. Those who do their home-work, invite themselves to meetings, and volunteer for extra assignments are the ones who become known as industrious, smart and capable.

If you want to be recognized, you must increase your visibility. The quickest and easiest way to learn is to ask a lot of questions of those who know. There are few people who are not flattered when asked their opinion or tapped for their knowledge. Pick someone you admire and ask if you can pick their brain on a subject in their area of expertise.

Having a 'go to' colleague in a different function or workgroup increases your organizational agility and provides you increased knowledge of how things work.

Internal company networking builds strong relationships and expands your circle of influence and awareness.

Approach your job more like an adventure and less like a means to an end. You will be amazed how much you will learn and grow by changing your approach and having fun with the experience. It is a choice and if you are going to spend 40+ hours at work, why not have fun and position yourself to make the most of your future?

Networking Advice from Networking Guru, Peter Biadasz

Due to the overwhelming request for information regarding how to effectively network, I contacted Peter Biadasz, author/speaker/publisher (networker extraordinaire), to request an interview.

In response to my question, "What 5 elements of networking would you suggest?" here is Peter's best advice:

- Know that you are a networker. This may sound funny or strange, but many people go to meetings not understanding that they are networkers. As a result they do not learn how to network and their networking is very ineffective. I was in the business world for many years before I understood that I was a networker and I had the poor results to show for it. As soon as I realized I was a networker and started learning how to be the best networker I could be, many positive things began to happen.
- Organize your network. When you go fishing you will catch many more fish if your net is strong with no holes in it, the same is true in networking. I once had a mentor who challenged me to list everyone I had known from high school to the present. He then had me

contact them to learn what they and their significant others were up to; and to let them know what I was doing. That was the start. Once your network is organized, add to it daily.
- Give a great 8 second intro. When you go to a network meeting you usually have a 30 or 60 second commercial built into the program. What they don't tell you is that studies show that you have about 8 seconds before your listener(s) decide if they want to continue to listen or not. Go to every network gathering prepared with a good, no great, way to get and keep the attention of others to help promote your business.
- Follow-up with everyone. When you meet people get their business card, take notes and follow-up within 24 hours. You may not transact business now, but maybe someone in your network may need them, or even better yet, maybe someone in their network may need your product or service in the future. Follow-up increases top of mind awareness.
- Start now. Why wait to receive the benefits of a professional networker? Know you are a networker, organize your network (the most difficult, yet, rewarding work you will ever do), prepare your introduction and follow-up on who you met today and even yesterday. Remember, it is net-working, not net-playing!

Bio: Peter Biadasz (pronounced bee-ahd-ish) is a graduate of Florida State University. His passion for and expertise in the area of people networking has benefited many for nearly two decades. Networking and the skills required to become a great networker are essential in reaching your next level of success. Peter has also been known to liven up his speaking engagments by utilizing his professional trumpet talent.

Peter has authored many books and is President of Total Publishing and Media in Tulsa, OK. You can find additional information about Peter and his books/resources on the following website: http://www.totalpublishingandmedia

11 Ways To Lose Your Job

We are all bombarded with hundreds of suggestions for keeping our jobs and making us indispensable to our employers. I love the positive approach to focusing on what works, as opposed to what doesn't. However, I thought I would shed some light on a few things that you might consider avoiding…unless, of course, you want to lose your job.

1. Take a personal call on your cell phone or text message during New Employee Orientation – or any time during work.
2. Have an intimate relationship with someone who reports to you. Better yet, flaunt it shamelessly on Facebook. If you are in Human Resources, it is not an option to enter into an intimate relationship with employees. Typically, this type of behavior will come back to haunt you compromising your credibility. Most importantly, it is the wrong thing to do.
3. Use Social Media to complain about your job and/or your boss. To really cinch the deal, use profanity – great for a very quick exit.
4. Call in sick, then text your friends at work from the mall or the beach. Surely, you don't think they will be excited for you as they are working responsibly.
5. Show up late every day, running in and dramatically explaining your daily excuse: grow up and plan your day like everyone else.

Experience Job Satisfaction

6. Show up late every day and sneak quietly into your chair – no, you are not invisible when you don't make eye contact.
7. For the two bullets above, the same goes for returning from lunch – chances are, your employer actually expects you to be working during the hours they are paying you.
8. Substance abuse at work – showing up to work under the influence, using at work, talking about using at work – enough said.
9. View, email, discuss, post in your cube/office, or show to your co-worker any form of inappropriate content – that includes pornography, inappropriate language, demeaning language…you get the picture. The email you use for work belongs to the company and they can pull your electronic history at any time and IT IS THE WRONG THING TO DO AT WORK.
10. Miss three consecutive deadlines blaming your co-workers. This may not result in an immediate dismissal, but it will shed such a negative light on you that you should begin a new job search as soon as possible.
11. Be a nasty, caustic, mean, sarcastic and generally miserable person. Nobody wants to work with, for, or have anyone around them who displays this type of behavior consistently. It might be time to find something you enjoy doing or, perhaps, work from home.

This Top 11 may seem like common sense to most of you, but these behaviors cripple careers every day and can be found in almost every company. You know who you are – stop it!

Are You Management Material?

In the hierarchy of all companies, each level and each position plays a critical role in the day-to-day success. If top leadership is effective, the leadership team is playing an inside/outside role navigating the waters of competition while looking ahead to make sure the company remains afloat and profitable.

One of the key players of the inner workings of companies is the manager. Managers keep all the plates spinning and use strong peripheral vision to ensure everyone is executing as planned for the desired results.

If companies support and execute succession planning, the manager roles may come open fairly often, as these people are developed to move up the organizational chart. As the manager roles come open, these are great opportunities for high potential employees to step into them. So, how do you position yourself to be poised for consideration for a manager position? Consider the following:

- Total commitment to the team is critical in demonstrating you are manager material. The most important aspect of being a GREAT manager is to understand how teams work and how to help them be successful. Seize every opportunity you have to bring your team together in your current projects. Supporting your peers will establish you as collaborative.

- Develop a reputation of integrity, credibility and respect by being consistent in what you say and what you do. Walking the talk will set you apart and position you as a person who can be relied upon. Reliability is a mainstay of great managers.
- Practice business detachment with co-workers/team members. Great managers do not have the luxury of becoming buddies with the people they manage outside of work. If you are viewed as a 'buddy' to your team, it could compromise your chances for management.
- Be consistent and fair. Managers are asked to make difficult decisions every day. Demonstrating that you possess a balanced perspective to do what is right, even in the face of opposition, will not only fair well for you personally, but professionally, as well.
- Managing change is what sets good managers apart from great managers. Find opportunities to support change efforts. Learn all you can about the change management process. You will learn from these experiences and show that you understand the nuances of management.

Taking advantage of local chamber of commerce events will allow you to network and build relationships with great managers to learn from and emulate. Develop a strategy for positioning yourself as 'manager material' by implementing what makes a great manager!

5 Reasons To Quit Your Job

Are there times when there are valid reasons to quit your job? As a career coach, my guidance is to secure a new position before quitting your old job. That being true, there are times when you have to walk away. Below is a list of what I believe to be situations that indicate launching an aggressive job search immediately!

1. Your employer is engaging in activity that is illegal, immoral and/or unethical. Nothing justifies these types of activities and you should leave as soon as you possibly can.
2. The culture supports mistreatment of people. This treatment is prevalent and systemic. There is great disparity between the treatment of people at the lower end of the company food chain and those at the top of the food chain. People are seen as expendable and bullying is not frowned upon.
3. Performance is not rewarded in any way. It isn't unusual for companies to be tightening the purse strings – in fact; they would be foolish not to today – however, there are many ways to demonstrate appreciation for performance. If your employer does not value those who perform and get results over those who don't – start looking.

Experience Job Satisfaction

4. The company is merely reacting to daily external pressure. If they do not have a strategy for the next 3 – 5 years, you should be very concerned that one day you will walk in and face being laid off. Many companies are struggling and fighting daily fires, but they are also thinking about the future of the company and planning for how they will fare when things turn around.
5. Communication is paramount to future success. If you hear nothing from the leadership of your company, there is reason for concern. Even in difficult times, strong companies understand the responsibility they have to their employees. If they NEVER communicate via email, management chain, town hall meetings, etc. ask questions. If you get no response and are encouraged not to ask – start your job search.

Even though the job market is tight, there are companies who are hiring. A job search will, most likely, take longer than it did five years ago, but this should enforce the urgency in beginning a search if you know you are in the wrong place. Take control of your own success and future. There are excellent companies who value talent, performance and people. These companies are fair and consistent in how they manage their finances, customers, internal stakeholders, quality, and employees.

Take Care Of You

For workers everywhere, the troubled economy can take a very serious emotional toll. Workforce reductions and reduced budgets have become common in the workplace, resulting in increased uncertainty, fear and stress. Because these issues are exacerbated in times of economic volatility, it's important to focus on more effective ways of coping with the pressure. Effective management of stress in the workplace may determine the difference between success and failure on the job. Emotions are contagious, and stress can affect the quality of your relationships. The more proficient you are at managing your own stress, the stronger your relationships will be with those around you and the less other people's stress will have a negative affect on you.

The Harvard Review published an article recently reflecting that job-related suicides have increased. It stated, *"The demographics of work-related suicide in 2008 resembled that of earlier years. 94% of work-related suicides were committed by men, and 36% were committed by workers between the ages of 45 and 54 — more than any other age group."*

The old adage, work to live, don't live to work, has never been as relevant as it is today. We have to remember we have a choice in how we manage our work life and how we prioritize our life in general. At the end of your career or life, do you want your legacy to be determined by how you handled your career or how you lived your life?

Experience Job Satisfaction

Equip yourself to best manage stress:

- Start moving – get out of your chair on a regular basis and walk around the office – take 30 minutes every day to take a walk from home – you will be amazed at how much better you will feel (certainly not new advice, but never more important)
- You are what you eat – make healthy choices and be moderate in the amount you eat – stress is one of the biggest contributors to obesity – don't allow the stress to define you!
- Get an adequate amount of sleep – new studies reveal we all are healthier and make better choices with 7 – 8 hours of sleep
- Volunteer – even if you only spend a small amount of time each month doing this, extending yourself to others offers many benefits to both the recipient of your time and to you

To avoid feeling overwhelmed at work:

- Begin your day by making a prioritized list of your daily objectives. Keep the list in a visible place where you can see it to avoid getting off track – time management is critical in times of stress
- Tackle large projects with a project plan broken into manageable mileposts. It is important to celebrate the successes along the way – this will increase motivation for the next step
- Utilize your resources – leveraging the talents of those around you will increase your strength and impact. Delegate when appropriate and ask for assistance, you are not alone.

- Emotions are contagious in the workplace - the best thing you can do for yourself is to remain aware of your behavior and the behavior of others. Understanding what motivates the way you respond to issues and other people will keep you in check and in control. Self-awareness is a powerful tool in all situations.

When all is said and done, a very powerful tool is a well-honed sense of humor. The ability to laugh at oneself, see humor in difficult situations and share this humor in your relationships will guard against negativity and allow for common sense to prevail. There are always choices, so make a conscious choice today to take care of you!

Are You Where You're Supposed To Be?

"A round man cannot be expected to fit in a square hole right away. He must have time to modify his shape."

Mark Twain

Culture Assimilation

While the job market is turbulent and unpredictable, there are people landing new jobs. As they join a new company, successfully assimilating into the new culture can make or break their career.

Entering a new company can be like relocating to a foreign country. New employees encounter new behaviors, dress, language, values, and rules. They will need to learn how to thrive among all of these in order to succeed and be a "good fit."

Underestimating the importance of cultural fit can be foolish. New employees are assessed for recognition, compensation, rewards and promotion, depending on how well they adjust in the new and, most likely, different culture.

Organizational culture is an unspoken value that, while intangible, if misunderstood or ignored, can manifest in negative tangible results.

The understood or informal rules, based on common values and beliefs, become the reality of how the work gets done. Those who join the organization are expected to adapt and accomplish their work in accordance with the culture.

If you are beginning a new position in a new company, below are a few questions you would be wise to explore early in your tenure:

What it's really like to work here?
What are the accepted behaviors and attitudes?
How do people communicate with one another?
How are decisions made and problems solved?
How are customers treated?
How is success defined here, and how does one succeed?
How do people work: independently or collaboratively?

From **Day One** on a new job, what will escalate and ease the transition is to quickly learn about the "way things are done here." How well a new employee "fits" is determined in the first few weeks, so learning the culture is as important as learning policies and procedures. In order to be successful, you must investigate, understand and comply with both formal and informal expectations.

The interesting aspect of cultural fit is that it is determined by people company-wide. There isn't one person or even one designated group of people who judge the fit. It is an organic behavior embedded in every company. When a new person enters the company, EVERYONE plays a part in deciding if they fit the culture.

All this being true, how do you begin conversations regarding the culture and whom do you ask? Networking is the best method to learn what is accepted and what isn't. Building relationships across the organization and demonstrating a sincere interest in how things work in the new company will position you as a team player who respects what is valued by others at the company.

New employees face many challenges when starting a new job: understanding your job, learning about your boss, figuring out how best to get along with new colleagues, etc. Make sure that understanding, respecting and assimilating into the culture is a top priority in order to be poised to reduce obstacles and escalate your success.

Tweets, Twibes And Tweeples

In the ever-changing landscape of technology, the rise of Social Media as a dominant force for communicating has penetrated every element of society. Can a virtual community possess a culture?

Every company and organization possesses a definable culture. Behaviors, decision-making models, intrinsic and extrinsic actions and how people are treated may all play a part in defining the culture. These elements of culture are measureable and easy to define within a controlled entity.

Social media lives and breathes in a virtual reality. It permeates all corners of the world, allows people to communicate across all traditional boundaries and thrives 24 hours/day. So…does it have a definable culture?

If you have spent any time on Twitter, you quickly realize thousands of people have a need to respond to the question, "What's happening?" Twitter has developed it's own language with tweets, retweets, tweeple, twitpics, twibes, etc. You can follow topics with a hashtag and people with lists. What is most apparent is the need people have to share.

The culture appears to be grounded in not only a need to share, but also a desire to be recognized. Retweets – when someone sends your tweet (message) out to their followers (a term supporting the need for recognition) somehow elevates your status within this community.

There are etiquette protocols as many people publicly thank you for following them and for retweeting.

Retweeting becomes a type of validation that what you are communicating is of value. Interesting, since it is unlikely you know anything about those you are following or those who follow you.

As you get deeper into the structure of Twitter, you can join a twibe or tweeple group, which provides inclusion – another indication that the need for recognition is systemic.

I often wonder if the need of those who Tweet to 'voice' runs parallel with their need to be heard. Certainly there are those who would deny this and claim they just want to throw out how they feel or think, regardless of being heard…much less understood. That seems counter-culture to what is evident in the virtual behavior exhibited.

It is cathartic to respond on Twitter to the question, "What's happening?" in the allowed 140 characters. They have provided structure and boundaries to respond within, which drives you to be forthright and succinct. Interesting that it feels uncontrolled, but is, obviously, very closely controlled.

At the end of the day, it is apparent there is a type of 'culture' within Twitter and, most likely, within twibes and tweeple groups. There are protocols, etiquette and rules to follow. There are consequences to not adhering to the rules. Messages move quickly, and are lost seconds after they appear. Does need for recognition overshadow the fact that it only lasts a few seconds?

What is most apparent is our desire to share, be heard and, ultimately, understood. Could it be Social Media has taken us back to the future and the culture is grounded in historically traditional values? It is difficult to deny the power of words and our freedom to voice. It is comforting to know some things are constant and, in the fast-paced world we live in, there are some things that remain the same, regardless of the venue.

You're Fired!

The volatility in our economic landscape affects many aspects of our lives. Pick up any newspaper, click on any news site on the Internet or just listen to most any conversation in a coffee shop – the content is likely to focus on how lives are impacted by the economic downturn. As the dominos fall, often the result becomes very personal as individuals lose their jobs.

Job loss is considered one of the most devastating of life events comparable to divorce, serious illness, relocation and death. Going from point 'A': gainfully employed, to point 'B': no longer employed, is a very emotionally charged journey.

Rarely do people know they are losing their jobs ahead of time, which is a protocol I support. There is no easy way to communicate to someone that you are ending his or her livelihood. This creates a very difficult and tricky situation for both sides.

Recently, Forbes magazine interviewed Jeff Garber, founder of 360JobInterview.com, New York based job interview coaching company, about how best to do the worst job in the world – fire someone. In the article are outlined some very important tips to keep in mind as you prepare to notify someone he or she is no longer employed:

- Keep it short, clear and concise. The employee is stunned and not going to hear or remember everything you say to them. Do not engage in a

discussion of why or get into the details. The emotional nature of the conversation deems it be short and to the point.
- While it is important to have an outline of what to say, be mindful in not sounding too scripted. Otherwise, you can come off as robotic and cold.
- It is very important that you are empathetic and keep in mind this is not about you – it is all about the person to which you are delivering the bad news and what they need at that moment.

In addition to the Forbes article, here are a few things you might consider:

- It is important to remember that someone previously made the decision to hire this person. You might consider thanking them for their contributions.
- Most people will find it embarrassing and humiliating to have to return to their work areas to pack up their belongings immediately after. Allow them to quietly leave the building and call later to make an appointment to return for their personal items after hours. Unfortunately, there are those who may disrupt the workplace if they return and you don't want to run that risk.

The old school version of outplacement was costly and not always very effective. There are some cutting edge, cost effective outplacement companies available who are doing a tremendous job at assisting people in managing the transition. Many of these companies will come onsite for the notification meetings at no charge and meet with the employees immediately after they are notified. They provide help in preparing the employee on what to say to their families, let them know they are not alone through the process and assist them with a plan before walking out. These companies typically only charge you for the employees who choose to participate.

The most critical part of the notification meeting is to allow the employee to leave with dignity.

Once the notification meetings conclude, the next step must be communication meetings with your remaining employees. If a carefully planned communication is not rolled out immediately, the employees left behind may feel guilty and be concerned they are 'next'. It is very important to redirect the focus to the work at hand and the future.

These events are very difficult and they should be. If you get to a point where letting someone go is easy, you may need to re-think your position. It is important to plan carefully, be clear and to the point, remain empathetic and be mindful of the remaining employees as you take the next step forward.

Brick & Mortar vs. No Boundaries, Part 1

Take a look around. Companies are launching without the traditional "brick & mortar" boundaries. Impressive street addresses are being replaced with .com addresses. Boardrooms are being replaced with online meeting venues. Employees can work from anywhere they have wireless access and cell phone coverage. How is this shift in "how we do work" impacting the culture of a company?

Let me introduce you to Jeff Garber, CEO, and Dan Fedrizzi, COO, founders of http://www.360jobinterview.com. In response to the recent job losses across the country, they founded 360JI to provide affordable career services to job seekers worldwide. 360JI connects job seekers to 300+ top HR professionals representing over 55 industries for PERSONAL one-on-one career/interview coaching, as well as resume services. This array of services is provided live via Skype. The mission: *to help job seekers get noticed and get hired.*

Prior to 360JobInterview.com, Garber and Fedrizzi spent over 20 years in marketing and communications. Jeff has emerged as a spokesperson for job search challenges with recent interviews for national media, including: Forbes.com, The *Washington Times*, *Baltimore Sun*, *Atlanta Journal Constitution*, ABC-Baltimore, *Huffington Post*, FOX Baltimore and *Syracuse Post Standard*.

I was fortunate to have the opportunity to discuss with Jeff and Dan the cultural differences between "brick &

mortar" companies and "companies without boundaries." Below please find part one of my interview with Jeff Garber and Dan Fedrizzi.

Q. *How does the culture in a company without boundaries differ from a traditional brick and mortar company?*

Jeff: Our company, 360JobInterview.com, has many of the same organizational and interpersonal challenges any company has, as well as a set of unique challenges. Brick & mortar companies attract and collect all types of employees, some motivated and some not. Some employees in traditional companies need a taskmaster to make sure they show up on time and stay on task. In a traditional environment, some employees respond to "big brother" very well. If left to their own devices, they could be very lazy. Companies without boundaries attract people who are self-motivated; it is not a place for lazy folks. You must be focused and self-motivated to succeed.

Companies without boundaries require an entrepreneurial type of employee. Offices in companies without boundaries are environments people create for themselves. They must be able to work in a certain amount of isolation. However, with Skype, cell phones, and wireless technology, the connectivity is no different than if they had colleagues in the next cubicle.

This environment also requires people who are passionate about what they do. If you hate your job, you aren't going to be good in this environment because people who hate their jobs need to look at a clock. They come in at 8:00 o'clock and count down the hours until five o'clock. We work all hours of the day and night, depending on our personal preference.

Dan: There are various levels of constraints in a company without boundaries. I don't feel there is a defined culture, yet. We are blazing a trail with no defined patterns, as opposed to a traditional company, which has very structured patterns.

Working in a company without boundaries is still in its infancy and too new to make a good comparison. It is constantly changing. However, being a part of the beginning of new type of work environments is very exciting. It allows everyone to stretch his or her talent and ability to innovate. The environment itself fosters the need to look at things in a new way.

Q. What are the biggest challenges/advantages to a company without boundaries?

Jeff: *The advantages are:*

You get highly motivated colleagues who are passionate about what they do. Our employees appreciate the freedom and flexibility they have. If they aren't a morning person, they may plug-in a little bit later. If a person is a night owl, they may work well into the night. People tend to work longer hours, more days of the week and their response rate to communication is far better than traditional companies.

The reason is, in traditional companies, most employees check out mentally at 5:00 o'clock. They may check their phones and Blackberries, but they are not as responsive as those who work in our environment. Companies without boundaries value employees more highly than traditional companies. This is the result of being a more progressive type of company. You are asking people to think out of the box and you are much more receptive to what they bring to the party because it is not structured in the same way traditional companies are.

I would compare it to coloring a picture on a page. If you don't have an outline or border, you don't have the constraints to color inside them and you will be much more creative. In our world, this approach results in new products and services.

One of the greatest advantages is the ability to leverage the latest technology. For instance, you and I can have a conversation via Skype, be discussing a client and have the ability to add the client to the conversation. The technology allows an immediacy in communication and people tend to be much more accessible. As a result, we are much more productive.

The challenges are:

It isn't for everyone. If someone needs structure, this probably won't work. However, we create our own structure. You and I may be talking via Skype, having a cup of coffee, we just don't happen to be in the same room.

As a small company without boundaries, we are very agile and can operate on a bigger platform cultivating relationships through networking beyond our local boundaries.

Dan: The advantages are:

More free thinking takes place due to the flexibility and creativity of this type of environment. This environment also breeds growth, change and opportunity. You can work anywhere and any time in the way you choose. People who thrive in this environment tend to be much more productive, as well as open to new ideas and ways of working. The lack of structure opens people up to be much more creative. People are inspired and self-motivated in this type of environment.

A company without boundaries opens your ability to employ people anywhere in the world, as opposed to recruiting people from your own backyard. This easily increases the talent and expertise we have access to.

There is no need to travel to meetings. With Skype, you can be face-to-face anytime anywhere. This allows you to remain face-to-face without the financial cost and time of travel. You can be anywhere without unplugging from your work and still work on your own schedule. Face-to-face communication may never be replaced completely, but the need for it is much less in this environment.

The Challenges are:

Working with people in various time zones takes an adjustment. You must be aware of where people are when scheduling meetings. You must be more flexible when working in these types of environments.

People are still apprehensive about working in this type of environment. Change is the only thing you can count on. If you aren't changing, you aren't growing.

This is not the first time Jeff Garber and Dan Fedrizzi have pioneered a new landscape. They are known for setting their compass in directions beyond where others have gone. They had a vision that has taken innovative ideas to a place where society is positively influenced in tangible ways to address the needs of millions. 360JobInterview.com most recently launched a new service that is revolutionizing the way Human Resource departments work. This new service is http://www.360WorkForce.com.

Brick & Mortar vs. No Boundaries, Part 2

Jeff and Dan, they have dedicated their careers to pioneering new pathways to innovative solutions in advertising, marketing and, most recently, job interview preparation and professional staffing.

The focus of this interview is the comparison of the culture of traditional brick & mortar companies vs. companies without boundaries. Part 1 focused on the advantages and challenges of leading a company without boundaries. Part 2 will take a closer look at the intricacies of leading in a world where your team may be geographically located anywhere in the world and working in various time zones.

Q. How do you maintain cohesiveness in your team transcending geographies and time zones?

Jeff: We are all compelled to work together during conventional hours. It wouldn't be very helpful if I start my day at noon and you start yours at 8:00AM. I would not be accessible and neither would you. So, we calibrate our time zones based on everyone's needs.

In regards to cohesiveness, differences of opinion are going to happen whether you work in a 'brick & mortar' company or a 'company without boundaries'. It all depends on what patterns you work within. For instance, you and I exchange 3 – 6 emails per day and the tone is always friendly and the response rate typically within an hour. If we have a disagreement, the tone of the emails and response rate will most likely change indicating we have an issue. Therefore, the issues are the same, but the cues are different. Working in a company without boundaries requires you to shift the way you work together. I am a direct communicator. If there is a problem, I prefer to be direct and discuss the issue, then let it go. You do have to be clear in your written communication using email or Skype chat. If I'm a sarcastic person and it comes across in my writing and you don't know it is meant in good nature, there can be miscommunication. I have a rule of thumb, when dealing with someone in a professional setting; you need to be face-to-face at some point via Skype or in person in order to understand one another's personality.

Relationships are very important to our success. I recently read an article in a professional news journal that stated it is unprofessional to use smiley faces in professional communication. I disagree. I spent many years in a traditional corporate environment and understand the protocol required in that culture. However, in this environment you must find a way to convey the meaning behind your words. Icons can represent the nonverbal communication you are unable to 'see' in this environment. In my opinion, communication is stronger in a company without boundaries. In a traditional brick & mortar company, people tend to hide behind office doors and voice mail. In a company without boundaries, we tend to be much more accessible. Because we are all remotely located we respect the need to communicate.

Dan: I believe in a company without boundaries, we handle things differently. Rather than treating our employees as people who work for us, we tend to consider them as people we 'work with'. It is the nature of the beast. As we work independently, we are much more connected which breeds cohesiveness. The respect we have for

Experience Job Satisfaction

individual contribution allows us to come to the 'table' as trusted partners.

It isn't necessarily easier to work in this environment and does have different expectations. The people who choose to work in this environment are often much easier to work with. They are more flexible, more productive and more receptive to the ideas of others. People who work in companies without boundaries often are on 24/7 and it is impossible to hide – each person has a unique set of responsibilities that is critical and connected to everyone else.

Disagreements are fewer as there is more focus on the goal than personality differences. The time we use to interact is treated differently. Because we are not in the same location 8 hours per day, we use the time we have to talk or Skype face-to-face to the best possible use of time. That doesn't mean we are all business We care about each other and have very good relationships. We do spend less time on small talk. We hold each other accountable which puts a higher emphasis on individual contribution. We are engaged and accountable because we choose to be.

Q. How do you manage vision and purpose? In a traditional brick & mortar company the physical location may represent the culture and have information posted representing metrics, performance, values, etc. How do you replicate that, or do you?

Jeff: I don't think you manage vision and purpose any differently than in any other company. You can do weekly telephone calls. I stopped our weekly calls because I was doing all the talking. I prefer to talk to people one-on-one. If we need to bring someone into the conversation, we do so via conference call.

Conveying our company culture is done in a more subtle way. It's the tone of communication, the website, communication vehicles, etc. For the most part, our website becomes our home base, even though that sounds really strange. The colors, graphics, and tone define who we are. Those silly motivational posters with stock photos that state things like mission, leadership, and success – they don't create the culture. I would like to think our employees are self-motivated and would be insulted by that. If you worked for a Fortune 500 company up until two years ago, people would have snickered at a borderless company. They desired the powerful address on the letterhead. With what has happened in the economy, we have all seen the erosion of loyalty and the ruthlessness in the way many large corporations behave. So now, we are actually the model for next generational business. Our employees feel if they work hard, we collectively can flourish and we do amazing things. Our employees feel more empowered and more secure. I believe our employees feel more in control because more is expected of them and more is respected of them.

As opposed to an impersonal large corporation, borderless companies are much more personal and relationship driven. Individual communication style is critical, as well as everyone's input in brainstorming. Honestly, after going this route, I would never want to work in a traditional environment again. I think it's too constraining.

I caution people who go into a borderless company thinking it is a way to have more time to themselves and work less. It is not the case and you will be found out quickly. The stigma has changed about working from home. You could be anywhere and be working. You really find out who is professional and who is not. Your professionalism is not determined by what time of day you work or what you're wearing. In a company without boundaries, your demeanor, as opposed to the corporate suit, determines your professionalism.

I believe companies like ours are changing how business operates and the mindset. I think this entire world is upside down and we are building something new. Those who cast their construction after yesteryear are in trouble. Those who break the mold and try to build, as opposed to re-build will be the innovators.

Dan: Vision and purpose are very important. We manage them much the same as any company. It is always crucial that vision and purpose are communicated and understood by your employees.

The culture of a company is something very difficult to manipulate, regardless of the type of company you work in. In a company without boundaries, the way the work flows and the lack of traditional structure creates a natural flow that evolved into the culture. I believe our culture is one of transparency and honesty. We hold everyone's voice as important and expect everyone to have a voice.

Traditional companies are often crippled by the structures they have constructed. Without those obstacles, we are free to move forward effortlessly and with great agility. Our culture is not a place for big egos or people who are controlling and not open to change. Adaptability is paramount to our success. If you have to 'see' a physical place in order to understand how to work in a company, this is not the place for you. Our employees understand we are measured by the work, not the well-appointed office.

Paving a new path is great, as long as it takes you to a new place of opportunity. We have a great team that is focused on new solutions and bringing them to those who need them as quickly as possible.

So, there you have it – straight from the mouths of those who are living the future today. One has to ask, if traditional companies eliminated the extremely expensive offices, what could they do to innovate new products…create more jobs…focus on the quality of the products and services they provide? Can you imagine a world where the hierarchy is eroded paving the way for individual contribution and creativity?

Be Fierce About Your Job Search

"Never wear a backward baseball cap to an interview unless applying for the job of umpire"

Dan Zevin

10 Updates To Improve Your Resume

Critiquing resumes is the #1 request I receive regarding job search coaching. Everyone takes a stab at putting into words their work history, accomplishments, awards, etc. and realizes there are a thousand different ways to do this and hundreds that are considered the 'best'. Is there a 'best' resume format? There is probably not just one, but there are millions of formats you should avoid. With so much information readily available, it is easy to become confused and overwhelmed. Let's face it; everyone wants the best possible resume they can create.

Due to the number of requests for help, I have put together what I believe are the best first steps in creating a strong resume.

1. Readability is critical. From the moment someone picks up your resume, presentation will make a huge difference. Font is important - please, please, please keep in mind – LESS IS MORE! Maintain consistency throughout with a clean, easy to read font. Use ONE font type and I strongly suggest Arial. I beg you to stop yourself from using different fonts throughout your resume; the interest should be in the content, not the font.
2. Avoid using underlines. They aren't interesting and add no value. Get rid of them.

3. When I work with clients to create content (the most important part of your resume) for strong bullet points, I take them through an exercise regarding utilizing their expertise, as a result of experience. At the end of the exercise, the raw data is developed into bullet points that are actionable and measureable. This is the most critical aspect of your resume. If you want to impress a future employer, demonstrate what you have done with measureable results. This will tell your interviewer you understand how to get things done.
4. What is the purpose of an objective statement on a resume? Do we really believe people need to be told we want to work for a growing company who values people and has opportunities for advancement? Take it off. It does not add value and can detract.
5. Along the same line as the useless objective statement, listing your strengths at the top of your resume, above your work history, is unnecessary and redundant. If you have strong bullet points and you have carefully considered what each of them tells the reader, you don't need them. In addition, people tend to use every buzzword they can muster in these lists. Demonstrate your strengths in what you have actually accomplished.
6. Be consistent regarding margins and formatting. Keep your content flush left, except for your bullet points. This will work to draw the reader's eye where you want it – to your strong actionable and measureable bullet points. I suggest this include your name and contact information at the top. Keeping it aligned flush left with the rest of your content will appear

Experience Job Satisfaction

clean and professional. This format may seem boring to you, but it will present you as consistent and organized, understanding what is important.

7. It is important to have a brief 2-sentence description of each employer in your work history. Don't assume this information is understood. It is important to state the size of the company (ex. Fortune 500, entrepreneurial start-up, large privately held, non-profit, etc.) In addition, add the industry, market segment, # employees...this can easily be found on their website. This tells the reader many things and demonstrates you understand the value of business acumen.

8. In regards to bolding text, I suggest bolding: name and contact information, company names, topic headings (i.e. Work History, Education, Awards, Civic/Volunteer Activities.) In addition, the most critical words to draw attention to by bolding text are the metrics in your bullet points demonstrating your results. If you have led an effort that resulted in 50% increase in something, bold '50% increase'. This will draw the reader's attention and keep them focused on what you are capable of achieving.

9. Use traditional bullets. This isn't about your ability to use MS Word; using more than one type of bullet looks silly. Stifle your desire to be creative in the formatting and use the simple, boring, traditional bullet. Let the interest lie in the content.

10. No longer is it the 'rule of thumb' to restrict your resume to one page. Use as many pages as it takes to demonstrate your experience and

expertise, just keep in mind if it gets too long, it better be VERY interesting. Try to reflect only the last 10 years work history. What you have gleaned from the last 10 years will impact what you can do for an employer today. This will keep you more current, as well.

I don't think I have to mention avoiding resume paper, scented or otherwise. I am well aware there are many who will have differing views on how to construct a resume to achieve the results you want. I happen to have a strong belief that your resume should be about you, what you have accomplished and what you have the ability to do in your next adventure.

Before You Enter An Interview, Arm Yourself With A Compelling Story

As we all know, the first question asked during an interview is often, "Please tell me about yourself" or "Please walk me through your resume from 10,000 feet." Many candidates walk into that room very nervous. As the competition for jobs continues to increase, the pressure to land a job follows suit. Due to the 'job interview' jitters or the pressure from competition, many candidates do not leverage what is their greatest opportunity to set the tone for the interview.

Many people take a very boring path by reiterating what is printed in their resume which any interviewer can easily read on his or her own time. If you begin the interview by neglecting to seize the opportunity to grab the interviewer's attention, you may have just crippled your chances of getting an offer.

While the question appears benign on the surface, what the interviewer is really seeking is the how, the why and the 'so what'. Once this question is on the table, the ball is in YOUR court and you have the opportunity to leverage this opportunity by telling a very compelling story that, if well articulated, will deliver your unique value in such a way to position you as the best possible candidate for that specific position. If done well, this will set the tone for the remainder of the interview.

Is this easy to do? Absolutely, not! However, if you subscribe to Stephen Covey's directive to begin with the end in mind, this is the opportunity to put this belief into practice. By walking through a process to determine what you want the interviewer to walk away with from the interview, you can use the information to create your 'story'.

With each position you have held, you should describe a lesson you learned, a success, why you left and how you applied your experience in the next situation. Demonstrated, quantifiable results tell the best story. Including examples of team interactions and opportunities you leveraged from experience (i.e. lessons, things you would have done differently, successes, etc.), will keep the interviewer on the edge of his or her seat.

If you can become confident and comfortable in telling your unique story (beginning-middle-end), you will be in a great position to establish a strong relationship with the interviewer. You will be less concerned by what you are going to say next and more focused on connecting personally. By embedding authentic examples based on your professional development, you will be poised to deliver what the interviewer is seeking. The end of the story should be a brief, well-organized wrap-up of how and why your experience, expertise and fit are perfect for the company.

Once you are comfortable in telling the story, your confidence will increase overall. Your story should be from 5 - 7 minutes long and never appear rehearsed.

The job market continues to yo-yo up and down. Until the landscape levels off and stabilizes, the competition for jobs will continue to escalate. The better you understand what you bring to the table, while increasing your confidence in presenting your value, the stronger your odds will be to land the job you desire.

Are The Unemployed Being Snubbed?

Not long ago I was inundated with emails from readers all over the country who are enraged over a recent series of online articles suggesting that smart companies will hire only candidates who are currently employed.

I opened my local newspaper yesterday (yes, I remain loyal to a paper newspaper I can 'feel') only to read an article about a Florida company who ran a job ad that originally stated, "No unemployed candidates will be considered at all." It was later revised to, "Candidates MUST be currently working for an original consumer electronics manufacturer in marketing. NO EXCEPTIONS." In the spirit of transparency, the company claimed it was a mistake and not their intent to omit the unemployed. Hey, they ran two ads with the same message, although softened in the second, and didn't retract until they received negative feedback. The message is clear.

Is this where we have arrived after one of the most turbulent economic times in the history of our country? Thousands of employees have been laid off in the last four years for a variety of reasons. Many of these people lost their jobs due to mismanagement of the companies they worked for and some due to the impact of the economic downturn – neither of which have anything to do with their talent or performance.

These articles and job ads would lead you to believe there is an assumption that ALL candidates who are unemployed are less desirable and were laid-off due to performance or some reason of which they had control.

I'm sure this approach is based on an assumption that the odds of landing the 'best' candidate are stronger if companies focus on employees who are currently working, rather than risk that an unemployed candidate is a low performer. However, in hundreds of instances, companies closed their doors for good and in other situations entire job functions were eliminated.

These events displaced thousands of people who are very talented and capable. Many of these employees were loyal to companies who were struggling and remained in support of these companies through very difficult times. These employees were displaced due to circumstances in which they had no control.

When you drown out the noise around this very emotion issue, it takes us back to a fundamental truth in staffing. Nothing is more important than hiring the RIGHT people and putting them in the right positions

Selection and sourcing are critical and take skill and expertise. Articulating clearly what you seek in a candidate, knowing where to source the right candidates and executing an interview model that will determine you have the right person will almost always prove successful. If you begin by narrowing your candidate pool on the premise of a bias that you cannot base on data, you will get what you seek – marginal results.

Let's hope most companies are wise enough to rise above this theory and execute a staffing strategy based on quality.

Strong Fit Or Misfit?

All the 'how to get a job' advice has finally made it's way around to focusing on 'fit'. If you peruse the social media sites for the 'up to the moment' information on what 'fit' means to you as a job seeker, you will find plenty of available information, but most is directed at the interviewer.

Can you creatively ascertain information useful to you, as a job seeker, from this advice? Maybe, but below are a few suggestion for taking control of your situation and deciding for yourself whether you are a good fit.

Beginning with the obvious – ask the question, "Can you describe the culture of your company, please?" If the interviewer freezes, struggles finding words to describe and won't look you in the eye – run!

If the interviewer alludes to the fact that lunches, office supplies and personal items often come up missing…blame is imposed for things gone wrong…people take credit for other's work…people are NOT supportive of one another (recipe for disaster) and communication never happens, you should be very cautious in moving forward. In environments like this, you will not be cared about, valued or developed.

Ask for a tour of the office. While your tour guide is escorting you, take a good look around. Do people look content, are they working, are they talking to one another, any smiles, how are they assessing the candidate who is being walked around?

Determine what type of culture that best fits your work style and ask more specific questions. In other words, if development opportunities are important to you, ask if they are available. If you want to be part of a strong team, ask about the work structure in which the position you are interviewing resides. If working in a collaborative environment is important to you, ask if collaboration is supported and encouraged. If the interviewer laughs and blows off the topic as something they are too busy to consider – beware.

Join local networking groups early in your job search. This will provide you access to people who may have great information regarding local companies and their culture.

This is certainly not an easy element of the workplace to determine during the pre-employment phase, but gathering as much information as you can will equip you to be poised for success. What you don't want is to find yourself seeking another job 6 months after your first day. Cultural fit is the #1 reason employees are released within the first year. Take control of your job search and cover all your bases.

15 Topics Smart Job Seekers Never Discuss…

- Having knowledge of something they clearly do not. Once you wander into this dangerous territory, you will always be asked to elaborate…deadly to the interview.
- Whether overtime is an expectation. What are you thinking? We all know companies desire people who are willing to work as long as it takes to get the job done. Even if you prefer not to, don't bring it up.
- How much they disliked their last position and/or company. Nobody wants to hear you criticize your former company.
- How much they disliked the people they worked with. See last bullet point. Companies want team players and people who are easy to work with.
- Personal problems. Quickest way to be shown the door.
- Health issues. Second quickest way to be shown the door.
- How many interviews they have bombed. Surely, this doesn't need explanation.
- How much the job pays. Wait until the interviewer introduces compensation. If you bring it up first, it can communicate you are only in it for the money.

- What can you do for me? (i.e. vacation, sick time, bonuses, etc.) This should be discussed once things get serious and when the interviewer initiates.
- Anything that includes slang or profanity. Be smart, act smart, speak smart.
- Anything that includes stereotypical language or language demonstrating a bias. Best to avoid being a liability in the interview: it will not reflect positively for you.
- Their life story. You are applying for a job, not therapy.
- The fact that they have no weaknesses. Everyone has weakness, if you pretend not to or truly believe you have none…it might be time for introspection and/or a reality check. Ask your friends and family, they are guaranteed to assist you in determining what you might improve.
- Anything related to conditions you require to be met in order for you to accept the position. YOU are the candidate. The interviewer has the power here, best not to threaten that fact.
- How much they need the job. Desperation is not appealing in a job interview. Try to appear confident and secure in the interview and during conversations with company representatives.

While these may appear to be information everyone would avoid, when you are in stressful situations you often allow your nervousness to dictate your behavior. It is always a good idea to remain aware of what to avoid before walking into an interview.

Define Yourself As A Leader

*"Do not follow where the path may lead.
Go instead where there is no path and leave a trail."*

Ralph Waldo Emerson

Leaders Who Coach

'Leadership' has been defined, re-defined and re-re-defined. While there are many ways to demonstrate leadership and as many different situations demanding even more hybrid applications of leadership, the fact is that in order for people to work in organized and efficient modes toward successful results, leadership is required.

In the context of the fast-paced, ever changing workplace of today, the most successful leaders are those who face new challenges with current and relevant solutions. Those who attempt to solve the issues of today with the solutions of yesterday may find themselves obsolete. That would be like trying to run the newest version of Excel on a 286 microprocessor.

One of the most successful approaches to the current demands is the style, 'leader as coach'. 'Leaders who coach' balance their concern with people performance with the goals of the company. The 'leader as coach' models the behavior desired by those around him or her. They serve as mentor and teacher allowing individual talent to flourish. They foster independence and accountability by exercising a high level of engagement. They often surround themselves with people as talented or more talented than they are and continue to develop them. Rather than being threatened by the talent of subordinates, they link arms and treat them as valued colleagues.

This type of leadership fosters a culture in which long-term performance is valued over short-term. The hierarchy is blurred with fewer levels of command replaced by a stronger informal network and increased communication between people. This builds a foundation of trust and inclusion. This type of leadership is nimble and agile in responding to change. This culture is prepared for the future to hold the unexpected in both threatening and opportunistic forms.

'Leaders who coach' are strong in adaptability and secure in their roles. They equip their people with the knowledge and tools they need to make sustainable decisions on their own. In these environments, performance and flexibility are a passion. These adaptive leaders value differences of opinion and encourage the healthy debate. As a result, employees feel valued and loyalty is the norm.

This type of leadership is certainly a contradiction at first glance. However, what these leaders know and understand is that in ever-changing environments, the best way to maintain control is to give it away. As they empower their employees, a more confident workforce emerges.

As we observe companies failing on a regular basis, organizations that are faced with instability and stress will suffer the same result as all other living things under the same circumstances, they must adapt to what they are faced with or they will become extinct. This elevates the necessity for agility and adaptability as the basis for survival.

Organizations being led by this type of leadership must have some very unique skills. Most employees must have the goal of becoming great problem solvers with well-honed decision-making skills within their areas of responsibility. The more volatile the environment, the less time there is to get final approval on every decision from the top. This requires that people be able to identify trends, principals and processes and feel confident in making decisions that advance the organization's objectives.

Organizations focused on the development and performance of all employees will create a common thread of organic knowledge transfer. Succession planning will develop as the natural result of talent management, as opposed to an annual structured event. Customer response time will increase as more ownership is fostered and expected.

No longer is the dictatorial 'command and control' leadership model effective in response to the challenges of today's workplace. Perhaps, we should begin identifying and developing leaders who coach for tomorrow's success. There are those who will claim this model will never work, that people must be controlled and told what to do. I challenge them to find talented people who desire an oppressive workplace.

This is certainly a shift that will take time and planning, as well as culture transformation. However, the investment today may provide ongoing success in the future.

Leadership For Growth

Regardless of whether you are CEO of a Fortune 100 company or an entrepreneur leading a handful of employees, to be truly effective you must possess an understanding of your leadership style and the effect it has on your organization. Your company can be highly successful on the financial side, with a forecast for tremendous growth, and still have a culture with low morale. Why should this matter to you?

The bottom line...sustainable success is driven by effective leadership. It is easy to get swept away when times are great and lose focus of the underlying framework (talent) supporting that success. When the economy turns around and jobs are more plentiful, unsatisfied employees will seek greener grass. Most companies have leaned down to the point that EVERY position is critical.

Turnover is not only costly financially, but can quickly create a talent gap that is difficult to fill. The longer the gap is open, the more risky the exposure. Companies void of strong leadership are especially vulnerable as the possibility of a mass exodus looms with the resurgence of open positions.

So, how does your leadership style measure up against the following criteria?

1. Acts with Humility

Nobody wants to work for a jerk. If you are self-obsessed and power hungry, you will become your own worst enemy. Understanding that YOU are not the business will equip you to be more objective. Otherwise, you will run the risk of creating a climate of fear and drive people to tell you what you want to hear, as opposed to the truth. Maintaining a balance of head and heart will keep your ego in check.

2. Stands Strong in the Face of Adversity

An effective leader validates information and knows whom best to surround himself/herself with to solve the problem. This, of course, requires you know where your talent lies. The leader then sets out to implement a plan with the help of his/her team. If additional problems are uncovered, the same process is repeated. Great leaders are relentless about finding the best solutions.

3. Constantly Supports Improvement

The companies most likely to survive, even when there are shifts that affect their industries, are the ones constantly focused on improvement. This culture of continual renewal, improvement, and learning starts at the top. Leaders who are constantly looking for ways to educate their employees, customers and suppliers remain open to better ways of doing things. They are less likely to fall into the trap, "This is the way we have always done things," which will lay a foundation for stagnation and, ultimately, their demise.

4. Is Fiscally Sound

One of the most common reasons for business failure is overspending. A very wise executive in the automotive industry once lived by the mantra, 'take care of the pennies and the dollars will take care of themselves'. His team heard this so much that every significant purchase was predicated by 'can we afford this?' or 'is there a way to do this without the expense?' This may seem a 'given' in our volatile economic climate, but we continue to witness business failure – large and small – due to mismanagement of finances. An effective leader is fiscally conservative when times are good and bad.

5. Communicates Consistently and with Clarity

Being a strong leader is not easy. However, one of the most important responsibilities of an effective leader is to effectively communicate. It is crucial that your messages match with your actions. You cannot state you care about employees and never engage with them. The success of your business is dependent upon your ability to communicate the strategy or vision of your company. In order for your employees to focus their efforts in the desired direction, they must understand what that direction looks like. Developing a compelling and inspiring message will motivate people to follow you.

6. Approachability

If you want to know what's really going on inside your business, you must be a leader to whom people are not afraid to give bad news. A predictable personality will send a message of security among your workforce. If you can balance your serious business behavior with a healthy sense of humor, you will create a culture of loyalty and honesty. Leaders earn employee trust by demonstrating respect and honesty. Great leaders are consistent in the way they communicate, which establishes a trust that is necessary in order to weather good times and difficult times.

The Framework Of Effective Leadership

Adlai Stevenson stated, "It's hard to lead a cavalry charge, if you think you look funny on a horse." Effective leadership is certainly not for everyone and those who find themselves in leadership roles understand the weight of the expectations and challenges.

Some leaders work their way into these roles with a planned effort demonstrating expertise and taking on efforts allowing them to shine. Others who would never strive to lead often find themselves with leadership responsibility thrust upon them. There is a school of thought that leaders are born and not bred. I'm not sure it's that clear cut and there are strong leaders who were groomed to lead early in their careers. Below are a few prerequisites and requirements in order for leadership to be successful.

As Adlai Stevenson was conveying, you must be confident and comfortable in a leadership role to dig in and take charge. If you are hesitant and second-guess yourself, you will compromise your role and the trust of those you lead.

Great leaders must see through a lens that reveals a vision that others are unable to see. Looking ahead allows for the current planning and strategy for a better tomorrow.

Effective leaders must lead with their ears open. They must practice excellent listening skills in order to hone in on what is critical and drown out superficial noise.

Otherwise, time and energy are wasted. True leaders are wise in knowing all voices at every level are important.

Exemplary leaders sense when something isn't right. You can say what you choose about intuition, but leaders who understand their employees, their business and the market will know something is awry before it makes itself known. This provides a unique advantage in a competitive marketplace.

Leaders who rise to the top are those who combine intellectual vision with an inspirational communication style. Head and heart are paramount to those who forge new paths, improve journeys and point us in directions we would not have taken otherwise.

Look around, if you have a leader who doesn't have followers – he/she isn't leading. The absolute most important strength for any leader is the ability to inspire others to follow. Without followers, a leader is completely void of power.

Born or bred, leaders are those we tie our lifelines to in the workplace. If you find yourself drawn to someone for guidance, are listening more closely to someone for wisdom and find yourself wondering what that person would do in difficult situations…you are in the presence of a leader.

Risks & Rewards Of Workplace Relationships

"Trust is the glue of life. It's the most essential ingredient in effective communication. It's the foundational principle that holds all relationships."

Stephen Covey

You Landed The Job! Now What?

So, you have submitted your resume hundreds of times via every mode possible. You have informed everyone you have ever known, including your many new 'best friends' on LinkedIn and Facebook, that you are seeking a new and challenging position. You have received just as many acknowledgments that your resume has been received – followed by, "Thank you for your interest. The response to our posting has been overwhelming and we have identified a candidate that is a stronger fit. We will keep your resume on file for six months."

Finally, you have a few interviews. The first are a little rough as you are out of practice, but by the tenth interview, you have perfected your performance. You have read all the tips and tricks and have found your rhythm in the interview process. However, there are thousands of job seekers and the competition for each individual position is fierce.

When you least expect it, you have a second interview and, finally, you get a call stating, "We would like to make you an offer." You try not to appear too eager (accepting on the spot before hearing the offer could appear a little eager) and realize you are on your way to having your life back.

You celebrate with family and friends and enjoy the euphoria for a few days. Suddenly, you realize you are beginning a new work-life. This will include new co-workers, new location, new expectations, new boss…in other words, you are facing a work-world unknown. Panic begins to set in and you find yourself worrying, once again. However, you do realize this is a good realm of concern and one you will work through to the other side. The real issue is getting off to the right start from the beginning.

Here are a few suggestions for making your new career journey a success:

- On day one current employees will assess you. Unfortunately, people form opinions quickly, so this is a great opportunity to present yourself as someone your new co-workers will want to work with. Smile, shake hands (firmly), repeat names back during the introductions. Ask them about what they do. Be sincere and listen carefully as they provide you information that will be valuable in the days to come. Hopefully, you have your work journal with you as this is a great time to take notes, such as names, titles, responsibilities, etc.
- Ask about the dress code before day one. Appearing like you are a good fit will position you as a good fit. If you have the opportunity, drive by the new office at quitting time and observe what people are wearing as they leave the building. Be careful not to lurk too long and appear as a stalker.
- Getting a lay of the land is important. Discovering the location of the coffee, restrooms, etc., is critical. People will be more helpful on day one and asking for their assistance during this discovery will allow you to begin building relationships.
- You will, hopefully, be thrust into New Employee Orientation on or shortly after day one. Pay attention, ask questions and get to know your fellow new employees. Being 'new'

together is a great platform for building relationships. Often, New Employee Orientation is the only time much of this information is presented to you. Take advantage of this time and gather as much information about benefits, policies and how this company does business as you can.
- Before you schlep your 'office-life paraphernalia' into your new cube/office, take a look around. While you are unique and becoming a mini-me of your boss or co-workers would be ridiculous, getting an idea of what norm looks like will go a long way in escalating your acceptance. As I am in and out of various companies as a consultant, it is clear each workplace has its own rules of what is acceptable regarding how you define your workspace. Be smart about this.
- On day one or soon after, you should have some time with your new boss. If you were not already provided the top three priorities for your position, this is the time to ask. This will demonstrate your interest, professionalism and seriousness about your new position. In addition, it will provide you important information you need to move forward successfully. This information is not always provided and by asking, you will prompt your boss to articulate the expectations and you will establish yourself as a good hire.

These few suggestions may seem small and a 'given' to many; however, there are people who are starting new jobs who haven't experience a 'first day' in many years. It helps to have a plan and moving forward with confidence will keep you in control of your future.

Dear Boss,

I appreciate working here and am thankful to have a job. I like the people I work with and care about them. I listen to you and try to please you when given the opportunity. Here is what I need you to know:

I'm not sure you are aware, but my name is Bob. I am married, my wife's name is Cheryl and we have a new baby girl. Her name is Zoe. We bought our first home this year, right before the death of my mother. You have never called me by my name or asked me about who I am. As a result, I don't feel like I matter.

When I am in your office to discuss work and you choose to type, read email and/or take phone calls, I don't feel like you are interested in what I'm saying. As a result, I don't feel valued.

When we launched the new product last Fall I was very excited. At my former company, we used cutting edge marketing strategies that were very successful. I emailed these to you as a suggestion, but you never replied. As a result, I felt invisible.

I have never been late to work. The only time I have missed work was two days for the birth of my daughter and three days when my mother passed away. I eat lunch at my desk and usually use this time to read and respond to my email. During the new product launch, I worked one to two hours late every day for three weeks and most Saturdays. I was not the only person working extra time for the success of the launch: the whole launch team put in many long

Experience Job Satisfaction

hours. You never recognized those of us on the team who put in the extra time to make the launch a success. As a result, we were de-motivated.

Due to financial constraints and the economy, we have downsized our employee population. Those of us who remain are expected to take up the slack and do more with fewer resources. My team has been meeting to explore the most effective way to get the work done and balance the workload. When we asked to meet with you to discuss our ideas, you were too busy. As a result, our team morale is very low.

The work our team did to make the product launch successful did not go unnoticed by our competition. As a result, I have been recruited to work for a competitor. The job offer is a promotion and has a higher starting salary. I realize I would not be afforded this opportunity if I had not been an integral part of the team here working on a high profile product. However, I don't feel the extra effort is appreciated. As a result, I am resigning.

If I chose to stay, I would run the risk of never being mentored or coached by an effective leader who is interested in developing the talent around which he/she is surrounded. I am worth more than that. I owe it to myself to do what is best for my family and my career. As a result, I have ensured these things are available at my new employer.

I wish the best for you and hope you discover that YOU are an important part of the process. You never really understood we were waiting for you to show up, we were waiting for you to lead.

Best regards,

Bob

Dear Bob,

I received your letter and wish you well in your new position. I regret my behavior contributed to your decision to resign. You are very talented and you will be missed.

While it is, obviously, after the fact, please accept my congratulations on the birth of your daughter and condolences on the passing of your mother. Please accept my apologies for not taking the time to do so previously. I do know your name. I may not have taken the time to get to know who you are, but I know what you are capable of and the tenacity you have to consistently raise the bar.

I am not excusing my behavior, but there are things I hope you can understand.

Like most mid-size companies, we are fire-fighting every day just to stay afloat. My focus has been solely on maximizing our most recent product launch and preparing for the next launch. If our department does not deliver and the next product launch isn't successful, everyone could lose their jobs. I was so concerned the fear I felt would permeate the group that I withdrew. As a result, I lost sight of the individual people I am entrusted to lead.

I mistakenly assumed all of you in the department understood how much I trust you and how important you are to me. Because I had complete confidence in your ability to do your jobs successfully, I focused on problems, not people. I did not take the time to recognize your efforts or success and share the pride I have in your abilities. As a result, you assumed I took you and your work for granted.

Early in my career, when I was about where you are, I was tagged a 'high potential'. I was selected to undergo a series of assessments and was put on the list for promotional opportunities. During the assessment feedback sessions, it was brought to my attention that I am an introvert. In addition, it revealed I have a tendency to avoid conflict. During my annual performance review, I was provided a development plan. The plan was designed to assist me in building stronger relationships, creating team cohesion and learning to manage conflict. Due to time, people, and financial constraints, the development plan was abandoned. I was fast-tracked and did not take it upon myself to strengthen those shortcomings. When I am under stress, I migrate where I am most comfortable – dealing with problems, technology, etc. As a result, I disengaged from you and the team.

I am well aware this is too little, too late. However, I hope you enter your next job knowing you are talented and you were valued…you just had a weak leader. Most importantly, please be sure you are 'running to' and not 'running from'.

Thank you for your honesty. I apologize for not showing up to be the leader you deserve.

Best regards,

Your former Boss

Generational Differences, Do They Matter?

I've been watching discussions on Twitter and other social media sites regarding the impact of a multigenerational workforce. I read one tweet claiming that Gen Y, Baby Boomer and Gen X mean nothing. The exchange went on to explain that the terms to describe the various generations were created by people to generate issues that are nonexistent. The source of this theory stated there was no impact regarding generational differences.

I have great appreciation and respect for all views, whether I agree or not. I think the freedom to believe as you choose is fundamental to who we are as individuals and you can see evidence of this on any social media site every minute of every day. You will also see the passion people have to 'voice' their thoughts, feelings and opinions. I often wonder if their need to 'voice' runs parallel with their need to be heard. I feel certain there are those who would deny this, that they just want to throw out how they feel, regardless of being heard…much less understood. It is cathartic to respond on Twitter to the question, "What are you doing?" in the allowed 140 characters. They have provided structure and boundaries to respond within, which drives you to be forthright and succinct. Interesting that it feels uncontrolled, but is, obviously, very closely controlled.

So, generational differences and the impact they may or may not have on a workforce. I think if you line up 10 employees ranging from 1-3 years of experience up to 15 – 20 years of experience, you will find dramatic differences.

The first difference that is evident is that the less experienced have grown up with technological advantages unknown in the formative years of those with 20+ years experience. They are adept at using technology and can leverage these talents in the workforce putting them light-years ahead. There are those with 20+ years experience who have kept up with technology, understand it, know how to use it and enjoy the advantages it has to offer. But if you listen carefully among a group of employees who represent both ends of this spectrum, those with 20+ years will defer to those at the lower end for their expertise. I personally believe this is how it is supposed to be and, if managed well, allows strong alliances to form as we rely on one another.

The group with more experience brings just that – more experience. They have made more mistakes and celebrated more success, so have had the opportunity to learn and adapt. They often have much more product knowledge, business acumen and historical data that are paramount in the 'big picture'. The wisdom that comes from experience is impossible to duplicate without putting the time in. This is exemplified as companies are scrambling to put Knowledge Management systems into place as we watch the Baby Boomers begin to retire. The impact of this generational migration could dramatically change the way we view the demographics of our workforce and what they bring to the table.

Do yourself a favor: accept the fact that all groups are needed and bring value. Develop work teams with diverse experiential demographics allowing a natural transfer of knowledge. Accept that each group feels they are the most important – probably a necessary attitude for success. Allow healthy debates on subjects from all areas and voices. At the end of the day, what rises from the debate will, most likely, be the best of both worlds.

To: Employees

From: Human Resources

It has been brought to our attention that there are misconceptions regarding the Human Resources group and we want to explain our role and intent.

It is not our intent to constantly throw the Policies and Procedures at you while policing you for lack of compliance. The Policies and Procedures are in place to maintain that the company is legally compliant, as well as ensuring consistency and fairness for employees as a whole.

We are aware that life happens to people and unexpected challenges may present themselves. We are here to listen, guide and offer suggestions within the parameters and scope of our influence/authority. It is our promise to you to maintain confidentiality, as long as what you reveal to u is not immoral, illegal or unethical.

Human Resources is a support function established as a part of the company foundation that keeps the business running every day. In that role, we act as a liaison between the employee population and management. This is, at times, a difficult role, but we must balance between the two to ensure both are equally represented.

As we are all aware, people are what keep the business running. It may sound like a cliché, but you are our most valuable asset. Due to this fact, it is critical that you are trained, developed and inspired to perform well every day in your role. We (HR) are here to link arms with you in the design and execution of your career development.

Please keep in mind there are financial constraints and we are not always able to provide the most expensive training available. That being true, there are many ways we can ensure you are getting the experiences that will equip you to move forward. Please have an open mind when we ask you to take on something outside the scope of your current position. It may be the opportunity that springboards you to the next level.

We (HR) sometimes have a reputation for being the people with whom you do not want to interact. We take this in stride knowing it is, in part, due to the fact that we have to make difficult decisions and maintain consistency. Often, it is our responsibility to deliver bad news and/or information you do not want to hear. Please know we do not enjoy knowing you would not choose to interact with us and hope you will allow us to build a strong relationship with each and every one of you.

If, at the end of the day, you take one thing away from this communication, we hope it is this: please know you can depend on us to keep you safe, provide you the best benefits the company can afford, be your advocate as the company navigates in a down economy and provide you individual assistance in each of your careers.

We take pride in our role and hope you will provide us the opportunity to support you.

Dysfunctional Boss, Part 1

Relationship skills are paramount to success both personally and professionally – certainly not new information. There are a myriad of relationships influencing our lives day in and day out. However, from the time we arrive at work in the morning until we head for home in the afternoon, the relationship that has the ability to make our lives productive or miserable is the one we have with our boss.

I, like most of you, have had many bosses in my career. I have had seasoned bosses and 'new-to-being-a-boss' bosses, quiet bosses and noisy bosses, bosses who were mature and others who needed a 'how to be a boss for idiots' guide, bosses who were great communicators and bosses who managed by osmosis…these have formed the model I either emulate or use as the bad example. In hindsight, these relationships are benign and I learned from the good, the bad and the ugly. On the other hand, while in the throws of these relationships, challenges arose that could have taken my career in a very different direction.

It would be impossible to outline all the different types of bosses and the pitfalls to avoid while working for them, but below are a few to consider if you find yourself challenged.

The Insecure Boss – this boss is a little paranoid, feels like he's out of the loop and something is going on behind his back. This is not uncommon for people 'new' to being a boss and who are accustomed to working as a team member where information is shared more readily. Being at the top often does not afford you ALL the day-to-day information. They haven't figured out that trusting your team is critical to successful management. The caution here is to avoid becoming the Insecure Boss's spy. Often the Insecure Boss will draw a team member in to use as his/her eyes and ears – while this may be an advantage to the boss, it won't be for you. You may believe it puts you in a more favorable position, but that is only an illusion. You do not want to be in this position. It can easily alienate you from your team, as well as your boss.

The 'Mums the Word' Boss – this boss holds all information close to the vest. There may be a vision and clear objectives for your team, but this boss is reluctant to share information, so there is a risk that the vision and objectives will be misunderstood. This type of leadership often has a desire for everyone to come to the same conclusion independently. Even in a perfect world, I'm not sure that's possible. They are the opposite of the micro-manager and this extreme provides no guidance. The risk here is becoming the interpreter. Informal leaders will often become so frustrated; they attempt to fill in the blanks. This type of boss will often allow a team member to step up and be the communicator. This boss may allow the interpreter to go down the wrong path and fail, which is a risk you don't want to take. In the current fast-paced workplace, this boss puts everyone at risk by not communicating.

The 'Best Friend' Boss – this could actually be the most deadly. This boss has a high affiliation need and meets this need by treating his/her team as buddies. This boss may pass on inappropriate company information to team members in an effort to appear 'in the know' and behaves more like a team member, instead of a boss. They are often uncomfortable in the 'boss' role and find themselves drifting back to where they are most secure. If a situation arises (and it always does) that requires the 'Best Friend'

Boss to reprimand a team member, their authority is compromised and they are ineffective. At the end of the day, they are not leading and the team will become insecure. The caution here is to avoid falling into the trap of becoming your boss' BFF. This isn't to be confused with the strong boss who is approachable and warm without compromising their position as leader.

These are a few boss/employee relationship pitfalls to avoid. Being aware of these is often all you need to be able to work within less than desirable situations effectively. Keep in mind it often takes a new manager time to assimilate to the position and many of these bosses have good intentions. By not succumbing to participate in unhealthy behaviors, these often work themselves out. If they don't, it may be time to seek a healthier work group.

Dysfunctional Boss/Employee Relationships, Part 2

Dysfunctional Boss/Employee Relationships, Part 1 received many requests for additional information, so today we will continue down the path of dysfunctional relationships between you and your boss.

The 'Unpredictable' Boss – when reporting to this boss, you never know who is going to show up. Some days he's approachable and engaged...the next day he's remote and dark. In most cases, these bosses are reactionary to external pressure and struggle maintaining a controlled front to their employees. The risk is their mood will permeate the team. The inconsistency will become systemic and the team will grow dependent on the boss to set the tone on a daily basis. This scenario will become distracting and can derail successful team efforts. As a team member, you have to be aware of this trap and stay in front of oncoming projects and pressure. In order to be effective, you have to be able to work independently as a team with guidance and consistency from your boss.

The 'Teflon' Boss – we all know this one – this boss is the great delegator. Nothing sticks to this boss. He/she will allow you to take on everything, take credit for your best efforts and no responsibility for those efforts that are less than stellar. He/she has a way of slipping through every loophole without accountability. This boss always has a smile on his/her face, can turn on the charm when necessary and can always talk the talk. If this boss has a strong team, it is very difficult to detect this flaw externally. The caution is to make sure you document every piece of work you do. This sounds like a 'CYA' scenario and it may be, but if you take on a project and it fails, you may not have any control as to how it is communicated outside your work group. It is important to document your work in all situations, especially this one.

The 'Phasing Out' Boss – this boss is tired. This boss has no desire to do more than necessary and is just biding time. Setting the bar or having a 'winning' attitude is long gone and he/she has no competitive spirit left to leverage. Obviously, this is not a great person to work for – especially, if you are a high performer/high potential. It will be difficult to convince this boss to let you take on more and he/she may not be supportive of cutting edge practices. You will not learn as much in this relationship and could develop some very bad habits. This is one I would recommend running from, if possible. If you are stuck in this situation for a while, remain aware of the pitfalls; seek additional support and alternative ways to continue to grow. Please note, there are superior bosses who have worked 20+ years: the length of service has nothing to do with this behavior. Many of the best bosses are experienced and leverage their experience as an advantage to continue to raise the bar. There are bosses at all levels who are low energy and have little interest in going above and beyond.

This concludes the list of dysfunctional boss/employee relationships. I encourage you to take control of your career and remain constantly aware of your relationships.

The Implications Of A Work Spouse, Part 1

'Work Spouse', an interesting term that can now be found in certain terminology resources...whether harmless or harmful, certainly an aspect of the workplace many fear to tread.

According to a recent study by the Vault, an on-line career and research source, 32% of the people they surveyed had a close relationship with a co-worker they recognized as a "work spouse." And just like a marriage, there are ups and downs, all between the hours of 8:00 – 5:00 - give or take a few hours.

We all know people who seem to share a 'special' platonic bond with a co-worker that, superficially, mirrors that of a marriage. They share inside jokes, seem to trust one another completely, finish each other's sentences and participate in knowing glances across the conference table.

One has to wonder when this phenomenon began and why. With people putting in more and more hours at work and fewer hours at home, could these hybrid relationships be filling in gaps due to the amount of time people spend together at work? Do they threaten the workplace in any way, as well as personal relationships outside of work? How can you protect your personal relationships from being negatively affected by your work spouse? All these are certainly related topics worth exploring. Below, we are going to determine if you, yes you, can be described as a work spouse.

Please be honest, at least with yourself, in considering the following:

1. You consistently rely on a certain co-worker for pens, post-its, mints, candy and over-the-counter medication.
2. You share inside jokes with the same certain co-worker.
3. You can be completely honest with this person about his or her appearance and hygiene (and vice versa).
4. When something newsworthy happens at work, this particular co-worker is the first person you seek out to discuss.
5. At breakfast, lunch and breaks, this certain co-worker knows what you like to order and how you like your coffee (and vice versa).
6. Do you feel giddy in discovering you and this particular co-worker are on the same team or project?
7. This certain co-worker knows almost as much about your personal life as your best friend or real-life spouse.

After reading the above, are you feeling uncomfortable? Have you answered 'YES' to more than one question? Is the information above extremely familiar? Do you feel the urge to send a text to your particular co-worker to tell him or her all about this article? YOU may be a WORK SPOUSE! (If you work with your actual marriage partner, this does not apply to you, please disregard.)

The Implications Of A Work Spouse, Part 2

Hopefully, *The Implications Of A Work Spouse, Part 2*, helped you define if you are, indeed, a work spouse. If you tested positive, this information may be of interest to you in managing this relationship. If you tested negative, this may enlighten you to the pitfalls, assist you in resisting the urge to participate or help you manage a team in which there is a work spouse relationship brewing.

First and foremost, take a step back and ensure your team members do not view the 'work spouse' relationship as exclusive. If they do, you run the risk of alienating others in your work team. This could be the demise of your success on this team and could bleed into your overall career. You should view all your work relationships as valuable and nurture each as you navigate your career. In an environment where the job market is tight, you should make every effort to protect your career.

Have you considered the way in which this relationship is viewed by those you report to or upper management? As we all know, there are no real secrets in most workplace environments and people love to spread something juicy, true or not. I doubt a work spouse relationship would be considered positive behavior if you are considered for a promotion. Perform risk assessment on your current situation to determine if it is worth compromising your career.

Everyone needs support and someone they can trust in the workplace. However, when the 'other' in this special relationship starts filling in the voids of an emotional need, you might consider backing off. Take responsibility for your own behavior and do what you know is right for you career...this is work, not home.

Consider what will happen if your 'work spouse' relationship ends badly. Again, it will, no doubt, be made public and embellished (probably not in a positive light.) It may easily become fodder for sophomoric humor and rightly so. How do you think this will affect your status, reputation and credibility?

Boundaries...setting them and keeping them are key in this situation. Beware how much you share with your work spouse regarding your personal life. If you have a real-life spouse or partner, this is not the vehicle to use for venting. In fact, out of respect for your real-life relationship, you should protect and maintain confidentiality above all.

We all have those we work with who we favor over others. It is human nature to gravitate toward people to whom we share commonality. These are actually critical to our success and often allow for honest feedback and support. We are all stronger when we link arms with those we work and combine our strengths for a common goal.

The work spouse relationship takes a one-on-one work relationship and redefines it as 'special' and exclusive. Make sure you foster healthy and authentic relationships at work, it will be worth the effort and provide you the platform you need to springboard to the next level.

About The Author

Teri Aulph is a graduate of the University of Oklahoma. Her passion for and expertise in people and how they interact with business have afforded her opportunities to make a difference on a global scale. Teri is the principal consultant at Teri Aulph Consulting, LLC. She has proven success in talent management, organizational development, change management and operational excellence. She has specific expertise in organizational design, leadership development and strategic people processes.

Teri has held executive positions as a global HR leader in Fortune 500 companies in various industries. As is evident in her writing, Teri believes people are the true key to any company's success. How every person's talent is utilized to ultimately create the best possible outcome enterprise-wide is where her passion lies.

As a global leader working within the space where the people and business intersect, Teri has earned a reputation as a leader providing People and Business Solutions through the sustained excellence of execution, for responsiveness, and for the wisdom of her counsel.

What sets Teri apart is her ability to provide cutting edge practices customized for her clients to meet their unique needs. Her primary role is to assist her clients in identifying challenges, developing an action plan and facilitating change for sustainable results.

Teri writes a career article for Examiner.com

http://www.examiner.com/career-coach-in-tulsa/teri-aulph

Teri also writes an article entitled, *Beyond The Cubicle: Corporate Culture* for The National Networker

http://www.thenationalnetworker.com

Please visit with Teri at:

http://www.teriaulph.com

Teri@teriaulph.com